TOWNSENDS

A SHOWMAN'S STORY

By Kay Townsend

CONTENTS

RICHARD TOWNSEND & SONS
FUN FAIR

ILMINSTER WILL VISIT CARNIVAL
OCT 5. 6. 7.

SUPER DODG'EMS · SWINGS
and a GREAT VARIETY OF FIRST CLASS
AMUSEMENTS

EVENINGS at 6.30   SATURDAYS at 2.30

4

INTRODUCTION

I come from a family of West Country showmen. When I was young, I loved listening to the old stories and found them so interesting that, when I was 11 years old, I made notes of all the things I did not want to forget. 36 years later when talking to a gentleman I told him one of those stories from years ago. He said, "Kay you must write this down, people want to know this." At the end of the summer season in 2004 I found myself starting to type and supposedly only doing this book for my family, especially the children. However, people have been asking, "When is it going to be finished? We would like a copy". So now I am doing this book for everyone. Every now and then you will come across 'Did You Knows?' which will contain interesting facts as you follow the story. I hope you find our story interesting and a pleasure to read. Therefore, with the help of my family, this is our showmans story for you.

CHAPTER 1

1829 – Our Beginning

On February 18th 1829,
at St Mary's Church,
Oxford,
the marriage of
Henry Townsend & Lydia Dixon.

To them was born a son
in September 1834 at Witney,
Oxfordshire.
They called him
William Townsend.

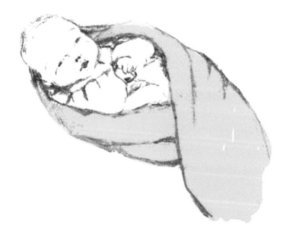

What We Know Of William's Life

William spent his childhood living in the High Street at Witney, Oxfordshire.

On 26th July 1856, he married a Miss Ann Ford, who was the daughter of a 'tucker' at a local blanket factory, and living in Corn Street. William and Ann were both 22 yrs old.

One year later their first child was born and they named him Joseph William. For the first few years of their married life the couple remained on Corn Street. Ann worked in the Witney blanket factory and William became a hawker, just like his father.

Four years later, according to the 1861 Somerset Census records, William and Ann had moved and were living in an old caravan at Christchurch Frome, Somerset. Now William was a travelling hawker.

By 1871 the National Census recorded that William and Ann, then both 37 years old, had moved again and were now a family with seven children. They all were living in an old caravan next door to the ironmongers near the Bell Inn pub in the market place at Radstock, near Bath.

William's occupation was described in the census as "Coachman/Carrier" on the Royal Mail stagecoach between Radstock and Bath, leaving daily at 8:30 am and returning at 4:30 pm. It is believed that Ann had become a china and glass dealer.

Circa 1800-1900 mail stage. Sketch by Carolyn Herbert.

By 1875 railways were more widespread and the mail was being transported by train, so William soon lost his job. William had very little money and the big worry was how he and his family would survive. The profits from selling a little glass and china would not have been enough to keep them all.

He came up with the idea of a small children's Round-a-bout. We are unsure as to whether he bought the ride (a juvenile ride to us) or if he made it himself. However, what we do know is this little Round-a-bout was to shape the next five generations of the Townsend family.

So William, with his little ride, actually started our journey of what was to become a showman's story.

8

Portland Fair

By now, William and Ann would have had two small caravans/wagons each being about 14ft long. The old wagons were made up of a single skin of thin board. Their children told later of how in the winter it was sometimes so cold they often woke up to find frost on their blankets! Their cooking would have been done outside on a fire, as the wagons were mainly for sleeping in.

William's little ride was simple, nothing fancy and very basic; it packed on a cart, and was pulled by a horse. This horse also pulled the Round-a-bout around in order for the children to have their ride.

As for William's children, when travelling to the next fair, they had to walk behind the cart. Some of these events would have been local charter fairs, where horses and cattle were sold on the street.

William and Ann had nine children, one of whom was Richard and he eventually became my grandfather. It is Richards's lifeline that this story will follow.

An early pony-driven Round-a-bout, in Oxfordshire
(By kind permission of the Fairground Heritage Trust).

Charter Fairs

William would have attended Charter Fairs with his little ride. These combination markets and fairs had existed for hundreds of years after being awarded a Royal Charter by the King reigning at the time of the fair's early years. The dates these fairs were to be held on each year were stipulated in the charter and could not be changed. If for any reason one year is missed, and the fair does not take place on the date as stipulated in the rules, then the Charter is broken. That gives the local Council the option, should they so wish, to stop the fair ever taking place again. If a fair has become a nuisance in the eyes of the local Council, they have been known to take advantage of this by not allowing a fair to return in the future.

Although originally established for produce and livestock sales, these gatherings would, in due course, attract all sorts of amusements. They were set up around the perimeter of the market area, such as "side shows", Jesters, magicians, stilt-walkers, fire-eaters, gambling games and fortune-tellers, their stalls to draw the curious but they also attracted undesirables in the form of beggars and pickpockets. Over the years, many of these fairs would lose their produce markets as the side shows became the attractions.

When I was a child, we attended a Charter Fair held annually in the square at Beaminster, Dorset. However, after many years, the family decided not to hold the fair. We knew that once the decision was made that was the end of it, as the Council would not allow us to return.

Family History So Far

Henry Townsend
Occupation: Hawker
Married In 1829
Lydia Dixon

Their Son...

William Townsend
Born 1834
Married In 1856
Ann Ford
Became Travelling Hawker,
Mail Stage Driver,
Then Travelling Showman

Their Son...

(Next) Chapter Two
Richard Townsend
Born 1866, Showman.
(my grandfather)

CHAPTER 2

1866

From here this story concentrates on William & Ann's seventh child, Richard, who was my grandfather.

Richard Townsend was born in 1866 at Radstock, near Bath. He was the seventh of the nine children born to William and Ann Townsend.

We know very little of Richard's childhood. In the 1881 Census, William and Ann declared that all of their children were scholars, but I have my doubts about this being true due to the amount of travelling they did. Richard was unable to read or write and even in his teenage he could only just sign his name.

We know that, as a young man, Richard left home and joined a travelling Menagerie, which was a mixture of street entertainers, jugglers and performing animals.

However, he was not gone for long and when he returned home Richard built himself a stall and, later, a set of swingboats. Along with his father (William) he would open around Dorset and Somerset fairs, travelling with everything he had packed on a cart.

Ten years later, at the time of the 1891 Census, William and Ann were still travelling with their little ride and living at West Street, Bridport, Dorset. Both were now 46 years old and their son, Richard, now being 25, had his own swingboats, a shooter stall and a small barrel organ to provide a musical atmosphere when they were open.

When Richard Met Kate

In 1895, Richard, at the age of 29 and still at home with parents, opened with his swingboats behind the Quicksilver Mail pub in Yeovil, Somerset. The little organ at the time was playing the popular song 'Two Little Girls In Blue' and Richard happened to notice a young lady who was dressed in blue. Her name was Kate Forse, daughter of James Forse, a local landlord. Richard was able to talk to Kate for a while and, eventually, he met Kate's father.

James Forse got along well with Richard, always making him feel welcome, and soon Richard and Kate were courting. Kate was nineteen and was a Sunday School teacher with a good education.

In 1896, not long after the couple met, Kate's father died and so her life with Richard began.

At the start of their years together they had only Richard's swingboats and stall and, for a while, they still travelled the region attending various fairs with his parents. Around 1896, Richard was one of the first people to pull a horse and wagon onto the Bridport fairground. Years later he told a reporter from the Dorset Echo that he could also remember opening in Bridport when horses and cattle were sold on the pavements in West Street and Round-a-bouts were set up outside the Greyhound Hotel.

Whilst returning from the Isle of Portland annual fair, in 1899, their first child was born. Kate went into labour as they reached Wyke Regis. So James Richard Townsend was born 9th November 1899 in a small wagon at Foord's Corner, Wyke Regis, Weymouth.

First born, James Richard (was always known as Uncle Dick).

By the 1901 Census, Richard and Kate were still travelling with his father William, as the Census recorded, in Damers Road, Dorchester in two living vans; one occupied by William and Ann with their three daughters and the other by Richard and Kate with baby James who was then aged two.

Unfortunately, Kate was not happy as she was an educated woman and this caused conflict with Richard's family. After a family disagreement,

Richard and Kate decided to go it alone. When open at Bridport Fair, William told Richard, "We are going back to Lyme Regis after this fair".

Richard said "You can, but me and Kate are going to Weymouth." So, in about 1905 with what little they had pulled by a horse, they made their way to Weymouth. There they managed to rent a piece of land near Weymouth harbour (now a car park) in Commercial Road.

Over the next 50 years, with Kate's mind for business and Richard's hard work, they built up their business which was known as Richard Townsend & Sons, Amusement Caterers. They became well known and greatly respected by many people and built a life that shaped generations of the family to come.

After their first baby, James Richard, was born in November 1899, later to follow were:

Thomas William born in 1902 at
Swanage Cottage Hospital, costing them 10 shillings.

Hilda Kathleen, born 1905 and Albert John (nicknamed Pat),
born 1906 at Commercial Road, Weymouth.

Doris Linda, born 1911 at Newstead Road, Weymouth.

CHAPTER 3

Townsend's Galloping Horses.

1905 – Building A Business

From 1905, after Richard and Kate settled in Commercial Road Weymouth their business started to grow and they managed to buy their first ride. Richard realised that many sailors would come into Weymouth from the nearby Isle of Portland naval base and would be seeking more entertainment than just the little fair which the Townsend's had. There would be much more money to be made if they had a big riding machine so, in 1908, he bought a three-abreast 'Galloper' steam-powered roundabout from showman William Wilson. One of the problems Richard soon faced was that the sailors would nearly always go to a pub with their girlfriends and get a bit tipsy before coming to the fair. Then, when riding on the Gallopers they would climb the brass rods and try to get up in the rafters of the ride. As part of the operating mechanism was up there it was a dangerous game so, to stop their little game, Richard nailed chicken wire across the machine's top frames, which did the trick nicely!

At the time when Richard and Kate bought their first set of Gallopers the ride was probably at its peak of popularity. It was the central attraction of the fair with crowds of people in their 'Sunday best' clambering on to ride the ornately carved and painted wooden horses accompanied by happy music from the Gavioli organ. For one penny a pocket-full, children could buy paper confetti which they threw into the air when the ride was in motion. This all helped to create a wonderfully exciting atmosphere which they could only experience at the fair!

Their First

(Richard)

In 1909, they were able to buy their first traction engine.

Empress of the South. An 8 n.h.p Burrell, works no. 2562
(Not members of the Townsend family in this photo)

This steam traction engine was new to the Portland stone quarries but, being only a three-speed engine, she was found unsuitable for the work and came up for sale. Richard bought the engine and had her converted for fairground duties. She was christened *Empress of the South.*

On August 16th 1912, at the age of 78, Richard's father, William Townsend died. At the time, his wagon was in a field next to the silk factory at Sherborne, as he had just attended the fair. As soon as Richard received the news of his father's death he rode his horse 30 miles from Weymouth to Sherborne and had to arrange for his father to buried in the Sherborne Cemetery. Remember, it was William in Chapter One who started our story with his little ride.

1914 was a year that Kate and Richard would never forget as, in the January, Kate gave birth to what would be the last of their children; they were triplets - Joseph, Kate and Mona. In August, the First World War broke out, then the Government requisitioned the *Empress of the South* for essential war work.

The last born

(Triplets)

Joseph (Joe) Harold , Kate Ruby & Mona Pearl born January 1914 in their showman's wagon alongside the harbour in Commercial Road, Weymouth.

Joe was my father, seen here in centre being held by Nurse Honeybun.
However, the two girl triplets did not survive.

Joe

All their children were born in their living wagon, except for Tom.

The family would venture out from Commercial Road to local fairs and fetes but always return afterwards. We know that only days before the outbreak of the First world War they were open at a fete in Upwey, near Weymouth as a local newspaper's caption under a picture of people happily riding on Townsend's Gallopers at the event said, "Little did these people know that in two days time we would be at war". Due to the war leaving Commercial Road occasionally came to an end.

Empress of the South, after the War Department requisitioned her, seen here in 1914 helping at Wilton, Wiltshire.

The strange thing about this photo is that although she was requisitioned the canopy bears the name Nicholes. It is known that her ownership changed to W. Nicholes in 1916, which was during her requisition time. After the war she went back to the fairgrounds again, as it has been recorded that in 1920 she was travelling with W. Nicholes Chair-o-planes.

The Commercial Road yard served Richard and Kate well as it gave them a base from where they were able to raise their children - all 6 of them. As the local school was close-by in the aptly-named School Street, Kate wanted her children to have some sort of education like herself.

Their schooling cost was 2d a week (£2 in 2011 values), so all their children were taught how to read and write, although not with pen and paper - a slate board and chalk instead! Although I can remember my father, Joe, could read a newspaper and sign his name I never saw him write a letter to anyone.

By 1915 Richard and Kate's first-born son, James, was now sixteen and he went to Wilton with the 'Empress of the South'. Dick was not very good at getting up early and so he had many a telling-off. He eventually joined the Army to fight and, like many lads, he did not tell the truth about his age. He was wounded in the leg by a sniper not long after joining and for three days he was trapped on barbed wire before being found.

Determined to survive the hardships of the War, in April 1918, they applied to the town council to put a small Round-a-bout on Weymouth sands. This ride was to become a part of the resort's history. (More on this in chapter four).

1918

Now the war was over the family, being young, had managed to pull through it in one piece and there was some celebration, now that they were back in normal business again. Unfortunately, money was short as the economy struggled after the First World War and things were not the same as before. By the end of 1918 Dick, now recovered from his war injury, was 19 and it was discovered that he was going to be the artist of the family. So much of his time now would be spent decorating the rides.

It was around 1918 when Richard sold his first set of Gallopers to Joe Brewer (of South Wales) and the next ride he bought was from a Mr Ted Fear, of Bristol and this was a Switchback ride. However, Richard discovered, after paying cash for it, that Mr Fear still owed money to the ride's previous owner. Therefore, the ride turned out to be rather expensive, as Richard had to pay off the remaining debt. As with all showmen, their children had to help with the business. It was sometimes a hard life but they did have some good times, as I have heard my Uncle Tom recall. Like most children, they got up to all sorts. The two daughters of the family, Doris and Hilda, were both very beautiful. At fetes, they would enter competitions, such as the 'Most Beautiful Ankles', and Doris would usually win. At one fete they came across 'Count the notches on the stick' to win. Doris would distract the man by talking to him, while the other children counted the notches!

Doris

Hilda

RETURNING TO THE STEAM ENGINES

Townsend's owned another four steam engines over the next ten years: a small Garrett, works no.31110,
compound 5.5 ton, 4 nhp tractor named *St. Bernard* registration HT 2959 bought in 1938 and sold in 1943, (not to be confused with Dorchester-based showman Herbert's engine, also called *St Bernard*)
Burrell no.4057, a 7.5-ton compound 3-speed tractor *Jellicoe II* reg. PR 8184, Fowler no.12255, 5 nhp, 10 ton, named *Princess* reg. FX 7170 (the family converted her to a showman's engine and she was retired in 1946) and *Queen Mary,* Fowler no.15319 (more about *Princess* and *Queen Mary* in Chapter Five 'The Steam and Our Queen.')

Richard had owned the switchback ride for three years by now but having to pay off Mr Fear's debt meant that it had cost him dearly. Perhaps the family did not like the machine, as after only 3 years, he sold it. An advertisement from a 1921 'World's Fair'
FOR SALE
30ft switchback, made by Savages, Kings Lynn. 8 cars, seats 48 grown-up persons. All complete, without organ or trucks. Reason for selling, bought Gallopers.
Apply, R Townsend, Commercial Rd, Weymouth.

In 1921 Richard bought his last set of Gallopers from, it is believed, Studts of south Wales.

This machine was more ornate (as you can see from the photo) and was a Tidman & Co. set which was cut down from a four-abreast version to a three-abreast. Three years later, Richard acquired a new 61-key Verbeeck (London) organ in 1924, which must have been intended for use in the centre of this ride.

Around the same time Richard managed to purchase his next big ride; a set of 'Chair-o-planes'. These would have been steam driven by their traction engine. Together with the gallopers, the family now had two big riding machines.

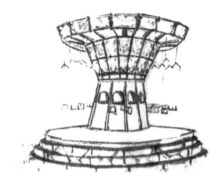

In the mid-1920s, it was decided to leave the Commercial Road yard for good and start travelling again but they would need to find somewhere to stay during the winter months. When the summer season was over a local farmer, Mr Symmons of Buckland Ripers, near Weymouth, would allow them to pull everything they had onto his farm. Whilst wintering there, another form of income was found for the winter season by cutting trees from nearby Tatton copse and selling the logs throughout the winter. Deliveries were made by horse and cart. Despite this, there were still times when they had little money but the farmer was good to them and allowed the family to help themselves to whatever vegetables were wanted from his fields. (Tom later said they were the happiest days of his life whilst staying in Buckland Ripers.)

Although the selling of the logs in the winter made only a small amount of money, you will see later (in Chapter Nine) that timber would become an important part of their lives. For now, everything was going well; they were far from 'well-off' but the money was slowly coming in again.

In the summer, the Townsends covered shows and fairs across four counties - Devon, Dorset, Somerset and Wiltshire - staying in villages or towns for their fetes and shows for up to a fortnight. They had also now acquired a Coconut Shy and, after all this time, still had their old Swingboats and Shooter stall. So, apart from having to keep the traction engine stoked-up to provide electricity for the lights, everyone else was taking money on something when open and they also had men working for them, as money-takers on the Gallopers.

One of the ways they would attract the punters to the fair was to buy a pig for ten shillings (£120 in 2011 values) and have a competition. Whoever sang the best song, and could hold the pig under their arm throughout the whole of the song, would win the pig. In order to hold the competition there had to be at least three contestants. The Galloper's steps were used as a stage and, it has been said that, if Richard found out who was going to sing he would take them to the pub first and get them a little tipsy! Thus, when they were singing and the pig would wriggle and squeal, they would drop the pig and so not win the competition. A pig would last quite a few weeks by doing this! Eventually someone would win and, with the excitement of it all, they would usually drop the pig and it would always run away. It was comical watching the winner run all around the field trying to catch his pig! I suppose that was part of the fun and why the punters always came. When open at Westonzoyland, a village in Somerset near Bridgwater, they decided to put on horse racing to draw the crowds but only one horse turned up, so they gave up on that idea!

They had other showmen join them with attractions. One family with their show would stand in front and call *"COME AND SEE THE THREE-LEGGED LADY WITH THREE LEGS UP TO HER THIGHS"*. Apparently, soldiers were only too eager to pay to see a girl with three legs and they entered the show with a big grin on their faces. However, their faces were a picture when they came out, as inside it was a female DUCK that had three legs. Then there was the fortune-teller, the punters thought it was unbelievable what she was saying which was unsurprising as she was drunk!
Another show that travelled with them was, "JIM BENNETT, THE MAN WITH TWO..." This got the punters curious; "TWO" of what? On paying their money and entering, they found it was a man with two thumbs.

Sometimes other families would travel with the Townsends. For a while, the Whitelegg family, 'Banjo' Edwards, Tommy Clemence, George and Flo Symmons, Charlie Connelly and Billy Hallett were just a few. They would all pay Richard a small pitch fee, as Richard would have to pay a farmer or the Council for the use of the field for the duration of the fair. However, if Richard saw the families had not done well he would waive the rent.

28

Whitelegg's shooter open with Townsend's fair at Dorchester, Dorset. The small table in the centre was for selling lemonade at 1 penny a glass.

Richard did not keep the Chair-o-planes for very long as, in the late 1920s while open at Chickerell, on the outskirts of Weymouth, a freak whirlwind blew the complete top off the ride and it was never found!. Very close-by is a stretch of water called the Fleet which flows out to sea so, we have always presumed, the top probably ended up floating in the English Channel! After this, they were down to only one big ride again, their faithful set of Gallopers.

What Happened To Our Gallopers?

The family know that one set of their Gallopers, (we do not know which set) possibly after our ownership, ended up at the Elstree Film Studios near London and was used in a movie. When the filming had finished the film company burnt the whole ride! We do not know the name of the film.

CHAPTER 4

1918 – Weymouth Sands

In 1918, nine months before the end of the First War, Richard and Kate came up with another idea. Richard approached Weymouth Council to ask if he could take a small children's Round-a-bout onto Weymouth sands. It was just a small hand-turned ride on its own, which consisted of small horses.

The first ride, circa 1918

In the Weymouth Council minutes from a meeting held in April 1918 it states:

Resolved: That permission be granted that Mr R Townsend to place a Round-a-bout on the sands as from Monday, May 13th at a weekly rent of £1.

At first, the Round-a-bout was situated near the Jubilee clock end of the beach then, later, it was moved to the Pavilion end. In those early years, as there was no shed in order to pack the ride away at night, Kate would take the little horses off the ride every evening, wrap them in blankets and bury in the sand. Each morning she would dig them up and put them back on the ride. Because the little Round-a-bout was doing well on the beach, Richard decided he also wanted swinging boats to stand beside the Round-a-bout, and this was the outcome:

Resolved: February 17th 1920. That Mr R Townsend be granted sites on the sands for juvenile Round-a-bout, and juvenile swings, as from and including Easter week, to the end of the season all at a rent of £160.

Notice the high increase in rent in such a short time (two years). In February 1923, the rent was increased to £200.

At first, he had six swingboats but these were later increased to eight. In the last chapter I mentioned that, in the mid-1920s, Richard had left Commercial Road and started to travel again with the Gallopers, in order to take more money. However, Kate did not travel but she stayed in Weymouth to look after the beach rides during the summer season, from May until September, while Richard travelled with the fair. To be close to the beach, Kate first rented a house in New Street but, eventually, she bought a house nearby at 1, Market Street. Sometime later, the first ride was replaced with this one (pictured below).

By kind permission of Weymouth Museum.

This ride was more sturdy, and larger, but was still was hand-turned at first. It had small horses and cockerels hung on twisted-brass rods which gently swung out as the ride turned. Its centre truck was on large cart spoke wooden wheels which, because they were old and rather delicate, the truck was transported to the beach each year on a flat, four-wheeled truck. First, wherever they decided the ride was going to be built, the sand would be scraped away until firm, wet sand was reached underneath. Then, two narrow trenches were dug in the wet sand, then old railway sleepers would be laid down in the small trench and the centre truck wheels would be pushed on to them.

This was for levelling purposes and to stop the wheels from sinking in the sand (*photo courtesy of Mr Gary Smart*).

No longer hand-turned, as electric power now being taken from a supply on the Esplanade. The 240 volts AC current would enter a transformer box near the ride and be stepped-down to 110 volts DC to the Round-a-bout by a wire buried very deep in a trench dug in the sand.

Townsend's kept a juvenile Round-a-bout on Weymouth beach for many years and only stopped doing so for a short time during the Second World War. Over the years, there have been three Mrs Townsend's on the beach. From 1918 until 1939 there was Kate;

Seen here in 1948, Frank and Lydia Townsend took over for the next twenty years.

In 1968, Pat and Phyllis Townsend were in charge.

Taken in 1978, my daughter Joe, then aged 3

Notice the little horses on the platforms in the picture above? These were off this ride originally, now with the brass rods removed, and blocks have been attached underneath on their bellies so we were able to continue using them on the ride by bolting them down to the platforms.

Six of these horses stayed on the ride in Weymouth and six went travelling with the fair on my father's ride. The horses are in retirement now and they remain in the family ownership today.

During the 1920s, a lady called Nancy Symonds would come to Weymouth with her grandchildren to sell fish. She would leave her grandchildren on the beach for Kate to look after. The children were well behaved and would sit by the promenade wall, waiting for their grandmother and when the Round-a-bout was not busy Kate would call them over to have a ride. This picture was taken when they were having one of those rides.

Memories, 1925

This picture was given to me by one of the children in the boat, (Mary) as a black, glass photo-plate; I knew there was something lovely behind it – as you can see I was right. The paintwork was by James (Uncle Dick.)
I know many people have childhood memories of rides on the beach, so Kate and Richards's idea back in 1918 became a part of Weymouth's history.

Did You Know?

Stakes

Normally, Swingboats have a stake at each leg as, when the boats are swinging up high, the legs need to be kept firmly fixed down. However, you cannot use stakes in sand as they would just slide out and not keep the leg secured.

Instead, a hole is dug in front of each leg and a ten-gallon can, which has been filled with sand, is buried with a chain attached to it and the leg of the ride.

The weight of the buried can then keeps the leg held down nicely.

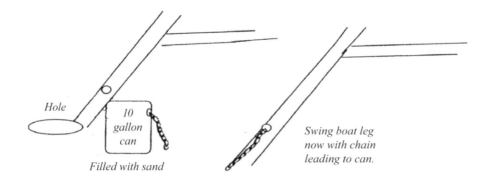

Hole
10 gallon can
Filled with sand
Swing boat leg now with chain leading to can.

I remember Uncle Tom telling me that on one occasion, whilst setting-up the Swingboats on a fairground, he hit a water-main while staking the ride down and water shot up out of the ground like a fountain! Years ago, when we attended the Charter Fair at the Square, Beaminster, Dorset we had small stakes especially made to keep the stalls down. In fact, that is what we called them, "the Beaminster stakes", as it was the only place we used them. These stakes had to be really short as under the surface of the car park there would have been electricity cables and water pipes. We were not popular with the local Council as, on the Monday morning after the fair, they would have to come and fill-in the little holes we had made all over the car park!

(however, we still had to use the long stakes for the Swinging Boats)

CHAPTER 5

1921-1948. Steam & Our 'Queen'

Water tank and empty coal sacks.
This horse and cart kept the engines going North Curry 1939
(Courtesy of Mr C Quick)

Richard and Kate Townsend had come a long way since owning their first engine, *Empress of the South*, in 1909.

'1921 Princess'

Fowler *Princess*. 12255, FX7170, was D2 class compound 5 nhp, weighing 10 tons. She is pictured here after suffering a broken axle whilst on the 28-mile journey from Axminster, Devon to Dorchester, Dorset. Above; Pat Townsend is on the far left

Built by the famous Leeds-based steam engine firm of John Fowler & Sons in 1910 as a road haulage loco and purchased by Richard around 1921. He converted her to showman's specifications (adding a dynamo, extended canopy and brass-work). She was used for towing the ride and living wagon

and run the stall lights from her dynamo when needed. The engine's powerful winch was used to pull out any trucks that were stuck on the showgrounds. Muddy fields are the one thing showmen can seldom avoid!

The *Princess* always towed the living-wagon and, for some years, James (Dick) the eldest, and Joe, the youngest of Richard's sons, would drive *Princess* on the road together. However, the two brothers did not get on well at all, so why on earth the family made them work together - especially on the road - we don't know. Dick and Joe would argue about some little thing and then stop the engine, get down and have a punch-up in the road! Then they would sit on the verge and refuse to get back on the engine with one another!

Meanwhile, away in front, *Queen Mary* and the rest of the family had pulled onto the new field. With travel being so slow, everyone was gasping for a cup of tea but the living wagon was with Dick and Joe who were now stopped on a road somewhere behind. For a number of years Richard kept a pony and cart and would drive back to find his boys and get them back together on the engine again. James and Joe were well known for their fights on the road, yet the family continued to put them together. We have often wondered why.

James (Dick) was the eldest and Joe the youngest

Allen Imber collection

In 1927 the road locomotive tax was doubled, from £30 to £60, which must have been a big shock to the family, when you consider they only charged 6d (six old pence a ride, so that meant a lot of riders were needed just to pay for the engine's road tax alone.

Princess 1934

I am pleased to say that *Princess* still exists today although no longer as a showman's engine, having been converted to a roadloco again by her present owners

40

Queen Mary

The 1929 Wall Street financial crash in America also affected much of Europe and Britain was really suffering by 1931, so the 'Depression' years were to be the next setback the Townsend family had to endure. Showmen found that the public now had little money to be spent at fairs but Richard still managed to keep everything on the road. Around 1931, he made an offer on two traction engines which came up for sale at a Portland quarry.

These were the last two engines that the family bought, One was originally called *Nellie* and *Polly*, these names were of two servant girls of the quarry owners who worked at their home, Pennsylvania Castle on the island. The asking price for these engines was £15 each, (£800 in 2011 values) but Uncle Tom offered them £25 for the pair and, two days later, the quarry sent a messenger to say the offer was accepted. Uncle Tom said later, "*So we only went to buy one but ended up with both*".

These engines had been hauling stone for quarry owner F J Barns. The engine named *Polly* was sold to another showman but *Nellie* was kept and became the family's favourite. She was built in 1918 by Fowler's in Leeds (works no. 15319) and registered in Dorset as FX 7850. *Nellie* was a 3-speed, 4-shaft engine and she had worked for the War Department before heading to the Portland quarries in 1921. Townsends purchased her from there around 1931 and on the day Uncle Dick went to collect her *Nellie* had been left in the bottom of a very steep quarry pit. Although she was rated at 7 nominal horse power (nhp) which was a reasonable size, a quarryman told James (Uncle Dick), "You have bought an engine you can't get out.

She will never pull up there, it's too steep!" Well, of course she did but only just!

Little did Nellie know here of the proud little showman's engine she was to become
(Courtesy of Portland Steam Rally)

The Birth of a Queen

So now *Nellie* needed to be converted to a showman's engine and here I must set the record straight. It has been written that the steam engineers Eddison's of Dorchester converted her to a showman's engine, but this is not exactly true. Eddisons did supply all the parts for the conversion but I was told the story of her rebuilding many times by my Uncle Tom. He and Uncle Dick spent all one winter converting her here in our village. *Nellie* was parked at Tidmoor Farm, on Chickerell Road, which belonged to a Mr Harry Andrews, and he supplied cups of hot cocoa while the men worked on the engine. Dick, being the fine painter of the family, decorated her with gold-leaf lining. From being a rather once-grubby quarry engine *Nellie,* with a new canopy, dynamo, polished twisted brass fittings and in our livery colours of maroon with gold lining, was now a sparkling showmans engine. All she needed was a name to match.

North Curry, Somerset 1939
(Reproduced by kind permission of the Surrey History Centre).

The family tended to name their transport after royalty and this engine was to be no exception. Tom chose *Queen Mary*, consort of the reigning monarch King George V, Uncle Tom was holding a bottle of 'milk stout' in his hand at the time, he smashed it against a rear wheel of the former *Nellie* and said, "There you are, I name you Queen Mary". So that is how our 'Queen' was born and she still exists today!

The family line up, with the 'Queen' towing

Around 1933 they decided to have all her brass-work chromed, including her wheel caps, which were so highly polished that a lady could see her face in them perfectly and could adjust her makeup, as one told me she actually did! Pender Plating in Poole carried out the work. After the job was done, however, the family agreed that the *Queen* had lost her looks and she was not right, so they had all the chrome removed and had her brass put back as before!

What She Needed

It is thought she weighs about 18 tons and her water tanks hold about 350 gallons.

When she was pulling a big load, the water tanks would take her about 20 miles before the next fill up, which would be drawn from a river or a spring and the family knew where every river or spring was for at least a 50-mile radius of Weymouth!

The speed limit when on open roads was about 12 m.p.h.

Before attempting to go downhill, they would have to stop at the top of the hill in order to put her in a low gear. Then, when on level road again, stop and change gear again. (No wonder travel was so slow!) Of course, there was supposed to be a spark-catcher on top of the chimney and the enginemen were always being told-off about this as they never had one! For a while, the police would stop the engine and make them put a bucket on the chimney top, which was a waste of time as, when the engine pulled away, the bucket would fly off! As they drove along the country roads, sparks from the chimney would sometimes cause small fires along the grass verge, so one of the men had to jump off the engine, and stamp out the flames!

Supplying Power at Night

The Gallopers had its own steam centre-engine which powered the ride so, at first, life was fairly easy for *Queen Mary*. During the first three years, the engine was only used for the towing on the road and supplying a little power for the lights at night. When other show-families travelled with them, they also would draw power from the *Queen* for the lights on their stalls and, at the end of the week, they would pay Richard a few pennies for the power. It was not until 1935, when the Gallopers were sold, that the

Queen had to really work hard as not only was she towing on the road, but also now supplying power at night for their new ride (see Chapter Seven) which needed 110 volts power, which the *Queen* supplied through her 300-amps Newton dynamo, which is still on her today. Her wire winch-rope was about 50 yards long, and it was once used when a tree was dangerously leaning over a house in the west Dorset village of Long Bredy when the family were asked if they would winch the tree away from the house. When supplying the power at night she would still use as much coal and water as if she was towing. When the ride was turned on you could hear the *Queen* loudly 'bark' as the ride pulled away, gaining speed.

The new Ark which the Queen *now had to run, pictured in 1935*

On Saturdays the fair would open at 12 o'clock and then close for about a hour at tea-time. By 5 o'clock the engine's firebox would be full of clinker (unburnt coal residue) and would need emptying before the start of the evening. In order to keep steam up, first they would top her boiler up with cold water to cool her, quickly shovel out all the clinker from the firebox until empty then throw in some sticks and a piece of paraffin-soaked rag which would fire her up again. Very little steam pressure was lost and she would be ready when the fair opened again at 6 o'clock. When the day was over, and it was time to close, one of the crew would climb up upon her canopy to put an old milk-churn lid over her chimney to stop the fire drawing during the night.

Denny, a cousin of the family, spent many years with us. He said that as a young man while they were open at Winfrith, a storm was brewing and Tom told him to dig a hole behind the 'Queen Mary and bury one end of the chain which they always had attached to her back coupling. This was just in case the Queen was struck by lightning during a storm. If she was not earthed, and they were open at the time, the dynamo could have been badly damaged and the strike could have killed Denny, or anyone, working on the engine. More about the Queen, her war days and the coal shortage in Chapter Eight.

When the family bought their first lorry (the Scammell) in 1946, the 'Queen Mary' was not sold immediately, but worked alongside their Scammell for two years. This was a chain-drive Scammell, which you will read more about in Chapter Eleven, so Queen Mary was not retired until 1948. Then she stood sheeted-over in the Putton Lane yard before returning to Portland under the ownership of Ken Coombes, who bought the Queen for preservation in 1950. Later, she was sold to Shropshire-based enthusiast Michael Salmon before coming back to Dorset when Keith Cook, of Horton near Wimborne bought Queen Mary in 1973. Whenever we see her today we still feel proud of her, as all showmen do of their old steam engines.

CHAPTER 6

1933 – Our Yard

In 1933 Kate decided that she no longer wanted to spend winters on someone else's land and said "I want somewhere for my children to live". She was able to buy a turnip field, called Queen's Meadow, in Putton Lane in Chickerell village near Weymouth. The field was about an acre in size, long and narrow and with one gate opening onto the road. The cost was about £100. In 1933, that was a lot of money to them but it was worth it as five generations of Townsends have lived here to this day.

The first winter they had to live with the mud as the turnips had been pulled leaving a ploughed field. They also purchased some large chicken sheds to use as work sheds for the Gallopers, as there were two fine painters in the family now, James (Uncle Dick) and Albert (Uncle Pat), both doing the paint work on the Gallopers ready for the following summer.

There were no sheds to house the traction engines so the water was drained from their tanks and each engine was covered completely in canvas sheets then bound tightly with rope to keep the winter elements at bay. Only once spring had arrived would the engines be unwrapped ready for the coming season. It was so muddy in the field during that winter when it had rained, that they bought Portland stone to use as a base layer. Next, thousands of red bricks were bought from the nearby Chickerell brickworks (delivered by horse and cart) then the bricks were neatly and tightly laid on top of the stone to create a brick road down through the centre of the long field. *Queen Mary* was stoked up and she was driven over the bricks so to press them firmly down. To this day, there are some of those bricks still in place. As Richard still had his pony and trap they also built a small, galvanized-iron shed as a stable for the horse.

During the Second World War, Weymouth saw many dog-fights in the skies as Royal Air Force planes tried to protect the coast from enemy attack. In 1941, it is believed a tracer-bullet from one of the aircraft went through the stable roof during one of those dog-fights.
It landed in a big canvas tilt which was hanging inside the stable. The family would sometimes hang the top tilts from the ride high in the roof to

keep them dry. For some time afterwards the tracer-bullet smouldered in the tilt and, consequently, the stable caught fire. It was daytime and only the women were in the yard at the time, so they sent for the men, who were cutting timber in Rempstone woods. By the time the men arrived home it was too late as the fire had destroyed the stable. Thankfully, there was no horse inside and no one was hurt.

Kate was a shrewd lady who had already been through one war and she knew prizes for the stalls would be in short supply during wartime. In preparation for the shortage, she bought tea-chests full of such things as glassware and chalk figurines, as you would win on a fair ground in the 1940s. Unfortunately, all the tea chests were being stored in the stable and were destroyed by the fire. They resorted to giving packs of five Woodbine-brand cigarettes as a prize instead and would collect old glass jars, filling them with bath salts. Woolworth stores were good for supplying prizes such as glass tumblers. The stable was soon rebuilt, using stone blocks this time, and it is still there to this day.

The Near Miss

The yard was never actually bombed during the war but it did have a near-miss one night when the family heard a bomb whistle as it went close overhead. They thought this was "it" for them but the bomb landed on the neighbouring farm at the end of the yard.

It was discovered the next morning that the farmer's horse was dead. He had been standing in the field but the shock of the blast made him fall on his knees and that is how the poor animal was found - his head lowered but he was still upright. When the farmer opened his barn door he found every animal was dead but did not have a single mark or wound on them. However, there was a cockerel that would roam freely from the farm to our yard and the blast had blown all his feathers off, so he looked as if he had been plucked! Apart from that, he was ok, just bald and still roaming around. Thankfully, none of my family were hurt and the only tragedy we had in our yard from the blast was Uncle Tom's little puppy, which was killed.

Now Taking Shape

It was not until the 1940s that the yard really started to take shape, when the family started to have wooden chalet-kitchens built next to the trailers so that in the winter they would spend the daytime in the chalets, for cooking and eating, only using the trailers for sleeping in at night. Now we had the chalets and in the 1950s we had the added luxury of television.

It was terrible when we had to pull out in the spring to start travelling again and leave the tv behind. This was before the battery-powered tv was even thought of and the only power we had in the summer was 110 volts DC, for the rides. Therefore, it was strictly television in the wintertime only. When we were away from the yard and mains electricity it was back to the Calor-gas lights again and having to sit directly under the light in order to read anything. I can remember I liked the smell of a newly-lit mantle and how warm and cosy the trailer would be with the small coal fire burning whilst the evening entertainment was listening to the radio. Now, of course, many years have passed and I look forward to being in the trailer where I feel more at home than being in the bungalow.

Back to the yard

In 1959 the big sheds were built, so the lorries and rides went under cover in the wintertime. The sheds are still there today, and I can remember my mother telling me, "*In 1959 we pulled out in the Spring as usual and we were away all summer open and, when we came back after Portland Fair, there they were all finished.*" Then, in the early 1960s, the first of the three family bungalows were built and the old wooden chalet-kitchens were demolished. So that turnip field that Kate bought back in 1933 became known as Townsend's Winter Quarters.

This photo was taken in the 1970s

CHAPTER 7

1934 – The New Ride

Townsend's Ark pictured on Weymouth Beach in 1953 for Queen Elizabeth II's Coronation celebrations

The Ark (pictured above) replaced the Gallopers in 1934. It was a big decision the family had to make to sell the Gallopers, as they had seen them through so much, but it was a matter of coming to terms with the fact that they had to move with the times to survive and the public wanted new, faster rides. Someone happened to have a Noah's Ark for sale, so Richard, Dick and Tom went to look at it but were too late as, when they arrived, it had just been sold. (Years later, Uncle Tom told me "It was just as well, because what we ended up with eventually was far better".) They had to decide what to do next and decided to go straight to the ride manufactures, Lakin & Co. of Streatham, south London to see if they could buy a new one. I asked my uncle what it was like when they arrived. He said *"There were wooden animals all over the place and it was a big open yard with men building an Ark for someone else. We went there and ordered ours in the December and it was ready for the spring, just right for the summer season."* The Ark was 42 feet (12.8 metres) in diameter with three animals on each platform section and 18 platforms altogether. Later, two of the platforms and their animals were removed and chariots added. The total cost of having the new Ark built in 1935 was £1,025.

After it was delivered to Weymouth, in order to try out the new machine it was built-up in the Putton Lane yard and for one whole day only, all the village children could come for as many free rides as they liked before the family pulled out for the summer season.

When it was new, the front top rounding-boards did not come with the ride but were bought from another showman (Smart's). They were blank and were finally fitted in 1944, while the family were open at Fairfields in Dorchester (now the Market car-park). The boards were 2 feet too long so, after trimming, had to have new irons attached in order to fit the ride. Finally, the rounding-boards were painted with the motorcycles, as pictured on the previous page, by Mr George Biles from Bridport, who also did much of the sign writing on the lorry doors. The bottom shutter boards had four different patterns of paintwork on them, over the years. When new, there were jungle scenes with tigers followed by, in later years, scenes of Scotland and then, finally, a design was painted on by James (Uncle Dick).

Original Outside Animals.

In 1963, twenty-nine years after they first bought the ride, the family updated the machine a little by removing the outside row of animals and replacing them with wooden motor bikes, which were bought from another showman, Bernard Cole at Southampton.

These bikes were stripped and repainted by Uncle Dick, Pat and cousin Paddy and a little chromework was added. In August 1963 they opened for the first time at what was to become one of their busiest venues - Weymouth Carnival. This was the first time that the newly-decorated motor bikes were used. Sadly, just a few days after the Weymouth Carnival that year, Kate and Richards first born James, (Uncle Dick) passed away aged 64, while they were at Sherborne for the carnival. Coincidently, James' grandfather, William Townsend (Chapter One) had also died at Sherborne, back in 1912.

Many other showmen cut and altered their Arks by turning them into Waltzers. When our Ark was sold and left the family in 1989, it was one of only a few still in its original condition. More on the Ark and the war in chapter eight.

(Courtesy of Mr R Spooner)

CHAPTER 8

1940 – The Second World War

On September 3rd 1939, war was declared between Britain and Germany. At the time Townsend's were open at Mere in Wiltshire and Police came to the fairground and told them that, now we were at war, they were to return home to Weymouth as the roads had to be kept clear for the Army. However, due to a lack of hostilities, this time became known as the "Phoney War". The Government was preparing for war but nothing really happened for several months, so the family lost the end of the season, during what we call 'the back end run', which mostly consists of carnivals. Other showmen did resume opening again just weeks after the announcement of war but Townsend's did not open again until 1943. All the family had to provide an income was timber work (which you can read more about in the next chapter).

In 1940 the war was starting to take its toll on the population. Before the war, many families enjoyed holidays at the seaside but now the beaches were part of the British defence system and most were strewn with barbed-wire fences in case of enemy invasion. So it was impossible to go in the sea or even on the beach. Even the small children's Round-a-bout on Weymouth beach (see Chapter Four) could not open and, along with the food, clothes and fuel rationing, the men being sent to fight, all this took its toll on the nation.

In 1940, the Government came up with the "Holidays at Home" idea, having decided the nation needed its spirit lifting. Billy Butlin was summoned to Downing Street and told to encourage the showmen to open again.

In 1943 Richard, Kate and their daughters, Hilda and Doris, started travelling again and they had men working for them as well. They travelled with the Ark, Swingboats and the small, hand-turned children's ride (Juvenile) and stalls. Being wartime coconuts were not available so there was no coconut shy, instead it was "Touch-em's" (knock the pegs down). The prizes were packs of 5 Woodbine cigarettes or a drinking-glass or jar full of bath-salts. This is all they had, as remember (in Chapter Six, Our

Yard) how the stable burnt down and all the prizes, or 'swag', were destroyed. The family did not travel much the first year; in fact they only opened at five different places in total throughout the year, stopping for several weeks at each one.

Wartime restrictions on lighting meant no bright lights were allowed on fairgrounds at night. Some families had black-out cloths which shrouding their rides but Townsend's did not. The Ark, which had eighteen platform sections to make up its 42 feet (12.8m) diameter, had four large light bulbs, known as '300s' which, although the same shape as an average household light bulb, were four times larger in size. Then they were painted black but leaving a small circle on the bottom of the bulb clear so a small beam of light would shine down for the money-takers to see the coins. However, for some reason, these bulbs would not last long and it was presumed the paint was the cause, as the bulb must have been overheating. So, they started to use nothing but blue pigmy lights from then on, but they gave little light and the ride looked very dull. What did help was that the Government put all the clocks forward by two hours, so it did not get dark until late. If dusk fell early they had to close, due to not having black-out cloths, however 10pm was the curfew time for all fairs.

In 1943 the family's first place to open was Victoria Park, Salisbury in Wiltshire where they stayed for six weeks along with Henry Chipperfield and his Gallopers, also Humbys with their sweet stall.
The first journey after being closed for so long took two days, as the journey to Salisbury ended up being a nightmare. The *Queen Mary* and her load, which was the Ark platform truck, living wagon and small round a bout centre truck, was proceeding along Preston Road which is only about six miles from the yard, with Cousin Denny and Joe were riding on the drawbars as the brake boys, when the bolt on one of the steering chains fell out, consequently the engine jack knifed side ways pushing up the curb stones in a heap towards the hedge. The platform truck drawbar twisted, so the truck ended up beside the engine.

Tom was steering and Marshall Herbert was driving, whilst Kate was riding inside the living wagon, all was unscathed. However, Joe, who was sat between the engine and first truck, had his hand trapped. An axe was used to smash the wood to free his hand, but the flesh from down his thumb and half his palm was peeled back. Rag was wrapped around it, and the milkman who was passing at the time happened to be going pass the hospital, so Joe hitched a lift with the milkman. The chain bolt was replaced and the *Queen Mary* continued the journey, however not for long, as then the gudgeon/cross pin on the end of the big end came out. They searched up and down the road and could not find the bolt, only to discover it had fallen in the old oil tray. Soon after this when near Stourpain, the fire bars dropped into the ash pan, someone then returned to Eddisons at Dorchester and collected more bars for the repair. Early the next morning they resumed the journey. Joe joined them a few days later with his arm in a sling. Next problem was going to be coal.

As this was the first time they had opened since the war started there was little coal left for *Queen Mary*. They ordered some from the local railway station but no delivery came so, for several consecutive days, they continued to re-order. Then, just when all hope had been given up of getting a delivery the coal arrived, but each order placed over the previous days came at once - all fifteen tons of it! Now, ironically, they had a glut of fuel and some had to bagged-up and taken to the yard in Weymouth.

When the fair was finally opened, it proved that it was worth the wait for the coal, as the people came in their hundreds and the Ark was full every ride, all day long. From then on, wherever there was an Army camp Richard would be open close-by in towns such as Salisbury, Blandford, Wareham, Shaftesbury, behind the Bee Hive pub at Wimborne and, of course, Dorchester. When the soldiers were sent away to fight and business went quiet, the family would then move on to the next camp.

Whilst open at Blandford, the river Stour which flows through the town, burst its banks. As the family were pulling the Ark down it soon was standing in two feet of water and, as they lifted parts of the ride up from the ground, the wood blocks and packing used for levelling the ride, floated away.

Before the war, Townsend's had only travelled and opened in the summer months but in 1943, for the first time, the family stayed opened throughout the winter on Dorchester's Fairfield (now the Market car park) where they joined Herbert's Fair, which had already been open in the town since 1941. The fair opened every night but when the snow came, and it was just too cold to be outdoors, everyone closed and took the night off! At Christmas a big party was organised for the local children by the American soldiers stationed in the town. Alongside the fair was a big 'Bofors' anti-aircraft gun, which was for shooting down enemy planes when they were trapped in the searchlights. When it was firing, the gun was so loud that it was frightening. We can only imagine the awful sight this must have been next to a fair.
Whilst Uncle Tom and Tommy Herbert were at Dorchester they were also buying and selling old cars. So, there was the fairground on one side of the car park and car sales the other side.

The family spent so much time open in Dorchester during the winter that they were able to use a big building within the market place for painting and repairing the Ark. However, they had to have everything cleared out each Wednesday, as it was Market Day and the building was used for selling poultry. The hall still exists and it is now an auction room.

Townsend's were open at Dorchester at the beginning of June 1944. Business went quiet, as the soldiers were being sent away, preparing for what we now know as 'D-Day'. Business was so quiet that the family only opened at weekends.
Of course, throughout the war the traction engines were still being used and the family managed to stockpile some coal at the Weymouth yard for *Queen Mary* and *Princess* but usually railway stations were very good at providing supplies.
When open during this busy time and supplying the power to the Ark, *Queen Mary* would burn as much coal as if she was towing on the road as,

when the ride was switched on, you could hear the *Queen* puffing hard under the load on her dynamo.

This did cause problems with the music system which was an amplified record-player known as a 'Panatrope' in the Ark's pay-box.

At the moment the Ark was turned on and started moving, so the amperage from the *Queen's* dynamo dropped for a few seconds and so did the speed of the music! It sounded very funny but, eventually, they could not stand it any longer and fitted a small resistance in a belly box of the truck and this cured the music problem.

On one occasion while at Dorchester, the dynamo on Herbert's engine, *Majestic,* caught fire, so *Queen Mary* was pulled alongside her to help out by running their ride and stalls until repairs were done.

On the *Queen Mary* there always had to be someone on the footplate to keep her going during this busy time and, for many years, it was one of our cousins, Denny Cave, who I must thank for his help in compiling this information. On Saturdays they would open in the afternoon but, by the end of the afternoon, the *Queen's* firebox was full of clinker (unburnt coal residue). Now her boiler would be topped up with cold water to cool her a little and then the hot clinker would be quickly shovelled out of the firebox in to a metal bucket. Often, the shovel became so white-hot doing this that it was plunged into the water as well! Next, they would quickly throw a few sticks and paraffin-soaked rag into the firebox to light her up again before she lost much steam pressure.

When it was finally time to close at night an old milk-churn lid was placed over her chimney-top to stop the fire drawing.

Pictured at Bere Regis in 1944.

This is the little Round-a-bout from the beach which was mentioned in Chapter Four, Weymouth Sands. Due to Weymouth's wartime coastal defences, the ride was taken off the beach and was travelled instead.
I have been told it was a lovely feeling when the war was finally over and the Ark was lit with bright lights once again.

Remember me mentioning in Chapter Three, that the next important family trade would be timber? Well, the next chapter will tell you what the men of the family were up to.

CHAPTER 9

1940 Timber

In Chapter Three (Building a Business), I mentioned when living at Buckland Ripers, that the family were selling logs from a horse and cart in the winter months, for a little extra money while the Gallopers were closed and when in 1933 Kate bought the field in Putton Lane, the family continued selling the logs in the wintertime.

By 1940 they had been living in the yard in Putton Lane for seven years and they were still cutting and selling wood.

During the War wood would be needed for the war effort and my family must have approached the Government and offered their services as all four sons, James, Tom, Pat and Joe, plus cousin Denny Cave, were hauling the trees out of local woods for the Forestry Commission. Their in-laws were also with them, so there were actually seven members of the family away hauling wood. They worked in four different forests at various times from 1940 to 1945 such as Rempston, Stourpaine, and Whitechurch, and finally Lulworth. The family did not use *Queen Mary* or *Princess* for the work but they were used again in 1943 when the rest of the family started to open once more with the fair, travelling around the camps and opening at Dorchester. For the timer work two Foden steam wagons were acquired, one of which was called *Little Lady*, an 8-ton, 4 n.h.p "D" Type tractor No. 13444, built 1928.

Little Lady Photo John Reeves

The steam Fodens were needed for their winches, which were used to haul the felled trees up onto a flat, four-wheel timber trailer.

A Forestry Commission inspector would decide which trees were to be cut down and these were marked by scratching a large cross on the tree. Other Commission workers actually cut the trees down, so all my family had to do was haul them out whole. The largest of the trees came from the Weld Estate at Lulworth and their girth could be anything up to 8 feet (2.5m) wide. A tree of that size could take an entire day to cut and after it had been felled, all the branches were sawn off and cut into cord wood. The main trunk of the tree was not cut immediately but would be measured by the Forestry Commission. First the girth and then the length, so they could work out its cubic measurement which was recorded into a notebook and then a tag was fixed onto the base of the tree. These details were needed by the Forestry Commission so they knew what to charge the sawmill and, also, the lumberjacks were paid by the size of tree they had felled.

Timber was needed to make items such as 'duckboards', rifle butts, parts for landing-craft and coffins, to name just a few. The small, thinner trees were used for such as telegraph poles and these were things the country needed at lot of during the War years to replace those damaged in enemy air-raids. From the Lulworth Estate small ash trees were felled and these were for turned into propellers for Spitfires. First the men would pull the timber-carriage alongside, parallel to the fallen tree. Long timbers would be leant, leading from the ground to up to the carriage.

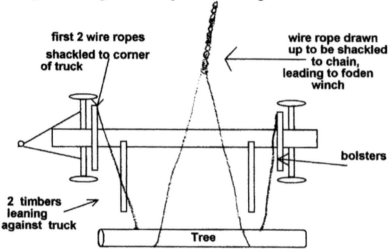

first 2 wire ropes
shackled to corner
of truck

wire rope drawn
up to be shackled
to chain,
leading to foden
winch

bolsters

2 timbers
leaning
against truck

Tree

Then wire rope would be wrapped around the tree leading to the winch and the tree would be rolled up on to the carriage. At either end of the carriages was a bolster, which could hold an 8 feet wide tree secure. The pole of the bolster would be pinned into place, preventing the tree from rolling off.

TREE PINNED
IN PLACE
BETWEEN
BOLSTER

These timber carriages were extendable, so they could carry the longest or the shortest of trees.

The family bought two petrol lorries; a Leyland 'Hippo' and a Bedford. The Bedford may have been a part-exchange, as Richard Townsend placed an advert in the September 1940 issue of *Commercial Motor* which offered "a Burrell compound steam tractor in good condition suitable for any work. "Will exchange for good Bedford lorry." The Bedford lorry was used to transport the timber to Sydenhams sawmills, in Poole. If Sydenhams had a glut of timber they would ask them to stop delivering for a few days but the men would carry on dragging the trees out and stack them in a field, ready to deliver later.

It was with the Bedford lorry, that the timber carriage turned over. Pat and Denny were in the cab after loading a tree, but they had not yet chained the tree on. They drove over an earth mound in the field and the tree slid sideways tipping the carriage and lorry on its side. The tools in the cab had fallen on Pat, everyone came running and thankfully no one was heart. The men climbed up out of the passenger door.

Whilst working in the forest, the men lived in an old 12 foot-long living wagon and a 6ft by 8ft shed.

All their cooking was done on two 'Primus' paraffin stoves, mostly by Uncle Pat. There was a special condition when working for the Commission,that the men were not allowed to return home to the fairground for more than 48 hours a week, as they were doing a job of "National Importance" for the Forestry Commission and were exempt from fighting. On weekends when they did return home it would be to wherever the rest of the family were open with the Ark and stalls. Then they would collect a large hamper full of cooked meats and fruit pies, which Hilda had cooked for them to take back to the woods. There were no fridges then so I am not sure how long the food would have lasted. There were no shortages of meat in the forest, as they would snare rabbits and shoot pigeon. Pigeon eggs tasted good, so I am told.

Winters would be very hard, as they would work through all weathers, rain, snow and stopping for nothing. A bowl of water left on the sideboard in the old wagon has been known to freeze over and their wet trousers worn from the previous day, would be frozen stiff by morning. Personal hygiene could be a problem, as the water tap would often freeze up so a paraffin-soaked rag would be wrapped around the tap and set alight to thaw it. Hot water for washing could be got from the Foden steam wagon's boiler, not that it would be very clean!

On "D-Day", 6th June 1944, the men watched Allied aircraft pass over the Lulworth Estate heading to France and the invasion beaches in Normandy.
On "VE Day", in May 1945, the men were still on the Weld Estate at Lulworth but, as soon as they heard the announcement that Britain was no longer at war, work stopped immediately. Uncle Dick, Tom, Pat and Joe were released from their duties and returned home to travelling again. The family were open with the fair at Dorchester at the time.
When the war with Japan ended on the 15th of August 1945 and it was Victory Over Japan (VJ) Day, Kate and Richard were open on Weymouth 'Marsh' an undeveloped area of land alongside the Weymouth - Portland railway embankment.
Despite the whole country having jubilant celebrations, the family still opened but no one can remember if they were busy or if people were in the mood for the fair ground. All I do know is that (my Dad) Joe and cousin Denny and Sam went to the 'Rock' pub to celebrate with the new beer called 'Stingo,' as hundreds of others did, but they got drunk and sleeping through whilst the rest of the family were open. Boy, did they get a telling-off the next day! followed by no one talking to them for days afterwards.

After the war ended, the family continued with timber work during the winter and they were cutting trees at Fleet, near Weymouth. In the early 1950's they found an ex-Army Mack lorry for sale. It had been working in an orchard in Somerset and it was bought to help drag out the timber (More on this lorry in Chapter 12). They continued during the winter months by buying another Bedford lorry and delivering bags of logs around the households in Weymouth for about the next 28 years.
My dad, Joe and Uncle Pat would leave the yard about 8.30 in the morning with the Bedford loaded up high with logs, returning about 4pm empty and then load the lorry up for the next morning. They would be out on the lorry five and half days a week and would only have Saturday afternoon off as on Sundays they would be in the big paint shed doing something to the rides, such as painting and repairing them ready for the summer season. Then, Monday morning, it was back on the log lorry again. They also sold large bags of 'nicky' or kindling wood.

I can remember, as a little girl, having to hold up the sack bags so my dad could fill them with the sticks of kindling. I hated doing it as my thumbs would be scratched by the sticks. When I was fed up in the yard, with no one to play with, I would go into the stable and sit on a big tree log we used as a seat, with a smaller block in front of me and chop the nicky-wood myself, through sheer boredom! So yes, I was chopping wood from a young age but, fortunately, never cut myself once, although I was not allowed to split the logs until I was 12!

For many years customers could buy bags of logs direct from our yard as well. Locals would wait until November, when we returned from travelling, and when our sign was out by the gate they knew we were back in business again, so would call in.

It was me who was the last member of our family to sell logs from the yard. After my mother died, in 1980, I decided the profit-margin was too low so I decided not to continue. After 50 years of the family doing timber, it was the end of an era in our family, but I never realised it at the time.

CHAPTER 10

1945 – The Boom

In Chapter Eight I mentioned how, during the War, the family opened again in 1943. At most places they were busy, taking good money and the war years became boom years for the showmen. So now it is 1945 and the War is finally over. For the last five years many things had been on ration, soldiers were being paid to fight, but there was little to spend their money on. There were very few luxuries to be had, food was short, and no holidays were taken, so some people were able to save a little money. Then, when the war in Europe was declared over, both Herbert's and Townsend's pulled out of Dorchester and went to Bridport to open, but returned for the home-coming celebrations. The soldiers came back home to their families and loved ones, and they were all given 'demob' money as well. So, there were many reasons for celebration - and boy, did they celebrate! Everyone decided to enjoy themselves by spending some of their money. There was little public entertainment to chose from and it was either the cinema, theatre or the fair. As a result, everywhere Townsend's opened they continued to do well. One such place was Portland Fair, held for two days every November and, as usual, other show families were open with their big rides too. At this particularly busy time, there were so many people that the rides were riding full every time. This boom-time really put showmen back on their feet again, financially. This boom lasted for the next five years until the country gradually returned to normal and luxuries became available again. Because money was now truly coming in the family decided to make the most of it and, in 1948 bought their next big ride which was a set of brand new Supercar 'Dodgems' (see Chapter Thirteen).

CHAPTER 11

1946 – Little Scammell

The Scammell 45 ton chain drive
(courtesy of the late Stuart Beaton collection).

We have progressed from the 1800s, when any fairground ride relied on horses for travelling until in came steam engines. Until now, the traction engines, *Queen Mary* and *Princess* had been towing everything on the road by day and supplying electric power at night but, for hauling, the traction engine were just too slow; it often took all day just to move from one place to another! In 1946, the family decided to retire *Princess*, as they now could afford to buy their first lorry for travelling, a chain-drive Scammell. We think she cost about £1,500 and when the family paid for her, it was not entirely with pound notes, but with loose change as well. They travelled by train to collect her, carrying suitcases full of half-crown and two shilling coins too! She was one of only ten 45-ton, chain driven Scammells that entered showland and had to be collected from Watford, Hertfordshire. Before a member of the family could leave the factory with her, they first had to drive on a practice pad, to show they were able to handle the lorry on the road.

1946. Feeling proud with the new Scammell, but with no body on her as yet

Sadly, they were not a good buy and showmen only found this out when it was too late. (They were not happy when the new Scammell 'Showtrac' came out soon after, which was better.) The Scammell was fetched while the family were at Dorchester Fairfields car park. Uncle (Marshal Herbert) drove her back but found it such a bad experience that he vowed never to drive her again! She was just a chassis cab when new, so the family had to add the body to her at a later date. She was plain grey in colour and came with her own toolbox which consisted of a spanner which fitted everything!

This is Mervin and Ivan House, who were felling the trees with my family (chapter 9). They later travelled with us, working on the fair.

At first, there was a lot of trouble with her fuel and it was discovered that the fuel tank had rust particles in it. Scammell's were contacted who said the reason was that they had made so many fuel tanks that they were stood around for a while before being fitted. The firm did not supply a new one but, instead, cousin Denny managed to clean the tank out - unfortunately giving himself dermatitis in doing so.

There were two drive-chains, one on either side, leading from the drive-shaft to the back axle. Her top speed was about 15 m.p.h., which was not a great improvement on the traction engine *Princess* but, due to the size of the two drive-sprockets and the thick chains, she was able to tow up to 45 tons.

This picture is of a Scammell with a 19-tooth sprocket, so by law she could tow 45 tons, three trailers, or up to 90 feet in length.

All our early lorries were named as the traction engines were, and

Vanguard

was the chosen name for our Scammell.

When it came to her engine reliability, without a doubt she was the best and she rarely let us down, with 6 LW 102 h.p engine. The Gardner diesel engine travelled about ten miles per gallon but the family still had to stop and fill up at streams every 20 miles, as they still had *Queen Mary* on the road. So, for two years, both traction engine and Scammell worked alongside one another. In 1946 Richard would buy something called "gas oil" for the Scammell, which was really diesel but, being tax-free, it was cheaper to buy, at only one shilling per gallon.

Eventually, the Government wanted more tax, so a red dye was added to mark it as tax-free fuel, but lorries had to be run on white diesel and the cost went up to half-a-crown (two shillings and sixpence) a gallon.

The Scammell had many drawbacks

Here are just a few. When we were in a muddy field, she would always get stuck. She did not like soft ground at all and had to be winched out many times. The ride was uncomfortable as the seats were just made of wood with a thin layer of horse-hair covered by leather. As Uncle Dick was short his legs were not long enough to reach the pedals so they put blocks on the pedals to make them higher up! The Scammell had four gears, plus reverse. When changing up from third to fourth, as long as you remembered to 'double de-clutch', you were ok. She was very low geared; so much so you could pull away in top gear. However, she had to be almost stopped in order to change into bottom gear before pulling a steep hill. There is one particular hill in Somerset called Wynyard's Gap, which is very steep and long, and towing two trucks up it would take about twenty minutes, sometimes longer!

Why there had to be Block-Boy

For the first few years there was a young man called Ralph Castleman who would ride on the open truck that was being towed behind. His job was to take care of the brakes on the two trucks when they were either about to climb a hill or go down one.

Early 1950s (courtesy of the Stuart Beaton collection)

When approaching the top of a hill, before she could go down the other side, Uncle Dick would give one toot on the horn. This would tell the block-boy to jump off the truck behind, while they were still moving (at about 3 m.p.h). The boy would run down one side of the load and apply the brake handles on both trucks, then the Scammell would be put into bottom or 'crawler' gear.

The brakes on the trucks would be kept 'on' down over the hill, in order to hold back the two trucks. This would help prevent the load from pushing the Scammell forward as the two trucks combined weight was more than that of the Scammell, itself being about seven tons.

When they were on level road again, two toots on the horn would tell the block-boy to let both the brake handle off again on both trucks.

After doing this, he would then run between the rear of the lorry and truck, which was still moving, climb up on to the high tow-bar and sit back on the truck being towed. (Can you imagine what Heath and Safety would say nowadays?!) By the time they had reach the bottom of the hill the brakes on the truck had become very hot and smelled so too! Going up hills, the Scammell was only a small lorry, so there was also the risk of her being pulled backwards. Therefore, they had to make sure she was in bottom gear before starting to pull. They could not risk slowing to a stop, in order to change gear, once they were so far up a hill, as she could have been pulled backwards by the combined weight of the two trucks. However, the block-boy always knew and there were blocks on the truck to quickly put behind the wheels if anything like this should happen. The Scammell brakes were the transmisson type and could not be used much, as they would become very hot and give off smoke up through the cab floor, so only when doing short stops was the foot brake really used. When approaching a junction, the driver would reduce speed, well in advance, and use very little foot brake. After a few years, the block-boy was no longer needed as the there was always a chap in the passenger seat to jump out if need be and much more powerful air brakes were fitted in late the 1950s.

Supplying the Power at Night

Before the family fitted her body a concrete ballast-block was put down into her floor to add weight and as a base to attach steel runners on to which a Phoenix 500 amp dynamo was bolted. The dynamo was to supply electric power to the rides and stalls at night and the Scammell was driven to Bath to collect it. At every new place we visited, the Scammell was driven on blocks to level her. Then, as she was chain-driven, two of her chains were removed and two narrower chains were led up from the driveshaft, inside the body, to two 7-inch sprockets, one on each side of the dynamo. Next, the Scammell would be put in fourth gear and by using a hand throttle, would run continually at approx 1,000 rpm. Driving the dynamo in the back which was then running at 500 rpm. The engine would run continually all day and night if needed. As I said earlier, when it came to her engine, she was the best.

In 1972, the Scammell went into retirement and remained under our sheds in the yard, covered over, for a few years. Until one of our other lorries let us down, so the Scammell was brought out of retirement for one summer only, then she was returned to the sheds again before being sold to a dealer in 1989. Then she seemed to disappear. Remember the Scammell had been with us for 43 years and we, the fourth Townsend generation had grown up with the lorry always being there, so we wondered what had happen to her? The family spread word that we were trying to trace her and for thirteen years nothing was heard. Then, in 2001, Mike Harris of London contacted us to say he had purchased her, so the family had finally found her again! She has since been purchased by a cousin.

CHAPTER 12

1948 – The Dodgem's

In 1948, as good money had been taken throughout the boom years (Chapter Ten), the family bought a brand-new set of Supercar Dodgem's and opened them, for the first time, at Sherborne in Dorset for the town's annual carnival. At the time, my mum and dad were courting and mum only lived six miles from Sherborne. One day, my dad said he could not see her the following evening as they were open with their new Dodgem's, so mum, being curious, caught a bus into the town to see the new ride. I remember her telling me, "When I arrived your dad was sat in the pay-box and your Uncle Tom and Uncle Pat were pushing the cars around the track with the riders in them!". The new Dodgem's had not been supplied with a top tilt (canvas cover) and on that first night it rained. Water on the track affected the contact of the cars' wheels on the metal floor-plates which was why Tom and Pat had to push the cars around. So their first night did not go at all well! Afterwards, another showman, Bernard Hill, loaned them his spare tilt while the family had one made. No transport came with the ride either, so two flat trucks for them were made by Sampson's of Dorchester. The Dodgem's floor was 60 feet (18.2m) long by 40 (12m) wide and consisted of 74 heavy metal plates with 22 pillars around the sides to support the top. The ride was only altered once and that was by lowering the top by six inches. I was told this was done because the pillars swayed in a strong wind. During the time we had them, they had one replacement set of floor-plates, which were delivered whilst open at Swanage. Although workmen from Supercar came and made the calculations, when the new floor arrived they were two plates out. I have since been told that Supercar's men were not very good at measuring!

In 1953, the Dodgem's and Ark were built-up on Weymouth sands as part of the Queen's coronation celebrations. It has to be said, however, that placing two big rides on a sandy beach was not one of the family's better ideas. Not only did they take little money but sand got into the small electric motors which were fitted inside each car. For some time afterwards, two or three of the motors were sent away each fortnight for the sand to be cleaned out. Only a few of them at a time could be spared, as the ride was in use every week at other carnivals. Until all the motors had been serviced, every time they were opened at a new place there were a few Dodgem cars missing, which meant less money would be taken. Townsends vowed never to take the Dodgem's on the sands again! After that mistake, the closest they ever came to the beach was in August 1963, when they made the first of many visits set-up by the Jubilee Clock on Weymouth Esplanade for the town's annual Carnival.

Each year at Sherborne, the Carnival Queen would be crowned on the fairground. They would use one of our flat platform trucks, putting a big blue cover over it, so that it looked like a nice stage. One year it rained, so kitchen chairs were arranged in a line along the centre of the Dodgem's track and the Carnival Queen was crowned there. Apparently, her dress and those of the attendants became blackened all around the bottom by the time they had finished! Unfortunately, the alloy dust could rarely be washed out.

Cousins Bernard and Denny in The Victory car.

In 1960, it was decided to have the cars repainted to freshen them up for the coming season and Mr Randall at Sutton Poyntz carried out the job, although not without a few problems. After removing all their little bonnets and spraying each part in three different colours, he went to reassemble them but found, that each bonnet would not fit just any car - each bonnet would only fit onto the one it had come off! Trying to match the bonnet colour to the rest of the car proved impossible and several had to be re-sprayed. Mr Randall's daughter, Suzy, would help the family when they were open at Bowleaze Cove, in Weymouth. Every Friday she would stand, barefoot, in a narrow stream which ran alongside the fair, called the River Jordan to fill buckets with water to wash the Dodgem's floor-plates. She hated doing this, as the river was full of eels and they would wriggle around her feet as she filled her buckets!

The water would be thrown across the track and then cleaned off with a rubber squeegie to remove any carbon deposits on the track.

Our Dodgem's floor-plates were made of alloy and were always black with carbon dust. I can remember my mother telling me how, one morning when I was a child, she dressed me in an all-white, brand-new outfit. Apparently, I looked beautiful in my little white pleated skirt. Then I made my way onto the Dodgem's track and, yes, the clothes were ruined with carbon dust! My mum said she had learned a lesson; never put me in white again!

As a child, I enjoyed playing with money and I can remember sitting in the pay box, on my Uncle Tom's lap, while we were open. He would allow me to stack the half-crowns and two-shilling pieces which the money takers had put on the counter in front of us, but I always would end up dropping some coins on the floor. My Uncle would then shout and throw me out of the pay box! Come the next place, I would be back in there, playing with the money again. Call it a silly thing to remember, but all showmen will have childhood memories which they will look back on and bring a smile to their face later in life - and what a care-free life it was too!

Portland Fair
Alan Imber photo

The top rounding boards did not come with the ride when new but were
bought in the 1960s from a showman called Teddy Morley and re-lettered
with the Townsend name

THE FLOOD

In July 1955, whilst open at Bowleaze Cove and right next to the sea, the
little River Jordan, running only yards away, burst its banks following
heavy rain. The deluge not only made the nearby holiday caravans float
along with their gas cylinders but also it flooded the fairground. The
Dodgem's thick metal floor-plates were lifted with the water despite each
plate being very heavy. It usually takes two strong men to lift one! A small
wooden bridge over the Jordan, which people crossed to get to the fair, was
washed away and the Army were called in from Wyke Regis Bridging
Camp and they built a temporary 'Bailey Bridge' until the old one was
replaced. Another casualty was Uncle Pat's "Hoopla" stall which washed
out to sea, never to be seen again! However, the game itself, along with the
rings and blocks which were in it, all washed up with the incoming tide
about a mile further along the beach - coincidentally, right where the other
part of the family business, the Swingboats and Round-a-bout, were set up
on Weymouth sands (see Chapter Seven). My Uncle Frank collected all the
rings and blocks and sent them back to the family at Bowleaze. Fortunately,

77

Uncle Pat found another Hoopla stall to put them in but the mud was so bad after the flooding that, until it was cleared, they could not open for few days.

Never again

In the 70s, the Dodgems were due to open in Pageant Gardens at Sherborne. On arrival it was discovered that trucks would not go through the narrow gate. Many of you could not understand what a task this was, when it was decided to carry every bit of the ride piece by piece through the gate, as at this time the cars had the fiber wheels (which are made up hundreds of layers of canvas). Tom's concerns were pushing the cars along the path to the track would damage the wheels, so two planks were put under the car and four men carried each car to the track, all twenty of them.

CHAPTER 13

1948 Goodbye Steam

In 1946 the family had bought their first lorry, a Scammell, and they also still had the *Queen Mary* for two years working alongside it.

After the War had ended, the family heard that the Army had surplus lorries, which were brought over here by the American troops but when they returned home to the States after the war they did not take the Mack lorries with them. Soon after the war, many ex-Army surplus items came up for sale at public auctions which many showmen attended, taking advantage of the bargains to be had. Ours came up for sale at the Middle Wallop (Hampshire) Army Auctions. The Mack the family successfully bid for was BTK 895. It was left-hand drive, being American-built, and was known as a 'Super 6', due to its 6-litre engine.

I remember Uncle Tom telling me years later, "It had air horns, but when we went to collect it they were gone. We could buy them separately for £20, which we did.". The Mack was like brand new, still with its delivery stickers on the windscreens and protective brown paper on the seats and hardly any miles on the clock.

Two things happened in 1948; the family bought a new set of Dodgems and retired their last traction engine *Queen Mary*, finally saying "Goodbye" to steam. However, just the Scammell on its own was not enough, so the

Mack was the replacement for the *Queen*. The Mack was bought in 1947 and went on the road in 1948. Its wheels were of the 1200/24 type and the tyres were impossible to buy in Britain, so they were changed to the 40/8's. The cab was canvas with half doors and was rebuilt by Ron Berry, a local carpenter in our village.

As usual, our transport was named after a ship and *The Leader* was the name chosen for this one.

The Leader BTK 895, Blandford, June 1968

You will notice the wheels were decorated with white paint. The family were renowned for all their equipment being well-maintained and painted, with red being our main livery colour. Apparently, white-wall tyres on cars and lorries were very much in fashion back then. The lorry doors were sign-written by Mr George Biles from Bridport. With its original, large 6-litre petrol engine, *The Leader* would travel at around three miles to a gallon and was notorious for its many breakdowns, usually with electrical ignition-coil problems. It also used to backfire a lot when going down hills! However, one thing can be said for this lorry, when she got going, boy did she move; in fact, whoever was driving her was told not to hold her back but let her go or, if not, she would burn even more petrol! Over the next 22 years, because she was so fast, *The Leader* would overtake all the lorries we had working alongside her and always pulled into the next place first. On the back of her was a chain-block on a high arm which was used for raising the Ark's centre-truck, in order to remove the wheels from beneath it when building the ride up.

(Courtesy of Mr G Smart)   *Using the chain block to lift Ark centre.*

BTK 895 Leader in 1973. She still exists.

Eventually, the family bought two generators from another showman, Edwards at Basingstoke, and these had 6LW Gardner engines and were ex-Navy mine-sweeper units, using a gallon of 'red diesel' per hour.

Photo Barry Brown

Garth, The Second Mack

Although the War was long over, the family still kept their timber business, cutting down trees in the winter and selling logs. Another lorry was needed to help with the work and, in the early 1950s, a second Mack was bought from an orchard owner at Hinton St George, Somerset. This one was also fitted with a new cab built by Ray Berry. She was eventually withdrawn from timber working in the late 1950s and then started to travel alongside the other Mack. Now the Townsends had one Scammell and two Macks on the road.

DFX 98 pictured in July 1967, named Garth. This lorry was eventually scrapped

Alan Imber photo

Its original petrol engine was replaced with a smaller, diesel one which improved the fuel consumption and the lorry would now return about 8 miles per gallon. The Gardner engine for this Mack came out of an old Scammell which, years before, had belonged the famous West Country amusement firm of Anderton and Rowland's. Changing the engine was not really successful as it made the lorry much slower, now the petrol motor had been replaced with a diesel one. There is a particularly long, steep hill in Somerset called Wynyard's Gap, which I have mentioned before, and the Scammell would take about twenty minutes to pull up it but the diesel-engined Mack took a lot longer. This meant that it was not much better than the old traction engine had been, as when she was put in 'crawler gear' she hardly moved. In fact, she was so slow that cousin Jimmy could get out of the cab, while she was still moving, and go into the pub, which is half-way up the hill and have a quick shandy! He then caught up with *Garth* and climbed back into the cab with her still moving through out the whole process!

For 22 years the Scammell and Macks were our main transport, plus one or two other lorries which joined in along the way; but that's another story. In 1972 the Scammell was retired leaving us without her dynamo for power when open. By now, the family had put the second generator on the back of *Garth* and then two more generators were made up. These two generators were fitted on the back of the Macks, so now both lorries had two power units, one of them on each being kept as a spare or back-up. Richard's motto was "You can never have too much power" and that is certainly one problem which my family never experienced - a ride closed down through lack of power.

In February 1972, during the national electricity strikes, Weymouth's GPO sorting office was having problem as their lights would going out when the postmen were trying to sort the mail just before delivery. The Post Office asked my family if they could hire the generators while the strikes were on and, as it was now winter and they were not needed for fairs, one of the Macks was driven to the Post Office yard in the town centre. Our generators produced 110 volts DC power for the rides and not the 240 volts AC supplied by the National Grid, so the main Post Office shop and the sorting office had to have our lights fixed to the ceilings as well! I was only thirteen years old at the time and, not knowing of the arrangement with my family, you can imagine the look on my face when I visited the Post Office in Weymouth, only to look up and see the lamp-battens off our ride on the ceiling!

We Had "C" Licences

As a child I can remember that, apart from the road-tax disc, there were "C licences" in our lorry windows. There were three types of disc available: "A" - to carry anything, anywhere; "B" - only within a certain radius and "C"- haul only your own goods. Hence we had to have "C" licences.

The Lorries Later To Follow

Albion Caledonian XAM 14, and was a ex-tanker.
We converted from 8 wheeler to 6-wheel tractor.

Akinson, 466RKO in 1987, Ex Farnell & Sons Parkstone.
Photo Barry Brown

ERF, Photo by Melcom Slater

We had a tractor too

Over a number of years, we kept a Ford D Major tractor, fitted with a powerful winch, and transported it around with us on a flat, four-wheeled trailer as in most years when we attended the 'back-end' (late summer/autumn) run of carnivals, there was often wet weather. Of course, we had mud too, so that we, and the other showman travelling with us, would get stuck in it and needed to be towed out of the fields. We always made sure that the other showmen along with us were not stranded either. Our tractor was also used to help get the centre-truck of the small Roundabout onto Weymouth beach (see Chapter Four) at the start of the season.

Photo courtesy of Mr N Haime

What was life was like on the road?

As I wrote in the beginning of this book, back in 1871 Ann and William were living in a small wagon and doing their cooking outside on a fire. It was a very cold life, but they took it in their stride as everyone did.

Before 1930, small tents called 'benders' were made with bent over ash poles and cloth thrown over to form a tent. These were built next to the living wagons for doing such as the washing, and cooking. All water had to be carried and then boiled up on a paraffin stove.

During the 1930s, the out-side tents disappeared, as more modern living-trailers came along with, at first, built-in cooking ranges then, later, Calor gas cookers. Now cooking was carried out inside but washing clothes was still done outside in an old bath with a scrubbing board. Sometimes you had to make it last, as there could be a restriction, such as you could only fill-up your water-cans from a tap at a certain time.

As Richard's children grew up, there were his sons and also men working for them, keeping everything on the road and families laundry could be a problem. At some villages, Kate would ask around and find a local woman who would do their washing. Each day a bundle of clothes would be delivered to her house and a clean lot would be collected later. In fact, when they were courting in 1946, dad would walk mum home with a bundle of dirty washing under his arm, as my maternal Grandmother did the washing for Kate when they were open at Milborne Port.

I am not sure what the women were paid in the village by the family for this service.

I remember, as a girl, putting buckets at each corner of our trailer in order to catch the rainwater, as it meant less water we had to carry for our laundry. Later permanent launderettes came along in towns and this made life a lot easier for us. We could not have washing machines, as the concept of plumbing in the ever-moving living trailers was not thought of until the 1980s. Then, of course, there is living with the mud. All showmen spend so much of the year in fields that the women have become experts at keeping mud under control inside. The women accept the mud as an unfortunate part of their lives!

Before mobile phones, the showman's contact was limited. Somebody once asked me what it was like when we were about to go on the road? Well, in our living-wagons any fragile things, such as china or glassware in cabinets, would be wrapped in towels or laid between blankets on the bed. Kitchen cupboards had to tied shut and we stood something in front of the doors to stop food or crockery from falling out. Water would be arranged by a showman in advance of the fair arriving but our water cans would be filled before going on the road, just in case the tap was not working at the new place on arrival. As there are no loft spaces in living-trailers, sentimental items are kept to a minimum. We certainly could not get our mail on a daily basis and letters were redirected to us each week by an aunt who knew where we were stopping.

If you were to ask me what a woman had to be in this life I would say a wife, mother, housekeeper, earner, business-partner and secretary! The husband is also the, earner, driver, painter, and repairer in all aspects - not forgetting his wife, who will be beside him through everything. That is probably why, in this business, there are few divorces, as the struggle of building their business life together makes a stronger marriage.

CHAPTER 14

1953 – Baker's Ground

For many years the annual two-day fair on the Isle of Portland was always held on November 5th and 6th and set out along the street through Chiswell, which runs alongside Chesil Beach. Richard attended this very popular fair for many years, right from being a young man. In the late 1940s, he heard that a piece of open land, known locally as Baker's Ground and situated right in the centre of Chiswell alongside the street had been repossessed from its owner by the Midland Bank and was available to rent from them. It was a prime spot to open for Portland Fair, so he rented Baker's Ground for a few years until, around 1953, when he had enough money to buy the freehold outright from the Bank. Originally, the land had belonged to the Church before a builder called Baker bought it and, from that time on, it was always known as Baker's Ground, no matter who owned it. Richard always opened there a few days before the official fair days began and then, as Portland Fair showmen gathered to set-up on the 4th, he dismantled the Ark and moved it further up Chiswell, rebuilding the machine on the street in time for the actual two Fair days, leaving the side stalls and someone else's ride in Bakers Ground. In later years the Ark was not moved for the fair days but remained on Baker's Ground.

You will see in the picture that the land was enclosed by a stone wall with three gates. This was ideal, as we would the gates so that the fair-goers could walk from the street fair into our part. It was an unusual (possibly unique) situation; the street was rented from the local council by another show family so, as we owned Baker's Ground, we were a fair within a fair. We always had to open a few days prior to Portland Fair itself, in order that we were then eligible to take part. Baker's Ground was owned by three generations of my family, the last being my two cousins, and me. In 2001, we finally decided to sell it. Today, where so many generations of people enjoyed sound and pleasure of the annual Portland Fair, there is a cluster of neat little houses called.... Baker's Ground.

Bakers Ground, Portland
(courtesy a Mr Andy White).

Two More Rides

In the early 1950s, a small Ferris wheel was added to the family rides. It was not a childrens' size (juvenile) and not your typical-size fairground wheel, but it was somewhere in-between. It could only hold a maximum of one adult and a child in each car, which was far from ideal. If there was too much weight in a car, the ride would only take its passengers up so far as the motor was not powerful enough to take them all the way round. This must have been embarrassing for whoever was in charge of it. In the 1960s, the ride was sold.

Portland Fair, November 1972

In 1967, the family bought an Octopus ride from the Jones Brothers and, whilst we owned this machine, a Leyland Hippo lorry was used to transport it. We did not use this ride much and in 1977 it was sold to Charles Cole. I have since been told that the ride was scrapped in 2004.

Blandford, 1972. The Leyland has now gone and it was the last year for our Scammell, seen here towing the Octopus.
Photos by Alan Imber

CHAPTER 15

1950 – 1960; Passed Away

In Chapter Three, I wrote of how Richard and Kate met when Richard was open with his father behind The Quicksilver Mail pub in Yeovil. In 1950, 54 years later, Kate passed away in her sleep, at home in the Putton Lane yard, Weymouth. In an obituary under the heading "The Perfect Partnership"

As a pretty young Sunday school teacher, and landlords daughter, she met and married Richard Townsend. They had 6 children, built a business surrounded by their children, and went through all the hardships of life together. They survived two World Wars and the Depression, and still came out on top. They were known and respected by many people; and together they built a life that that shaped the generations to come. The showland newspaper *The World's Fair* wrote,

"Mrs Townsend left the more active running of the Round-a-bouts to her husband and tended to the business and books side of the business. It was the perfect partnership between husband and wife."

1960 Ten Years Later

At the Chard spring fair, Richard had taken a fall down the wagon steps and was not himself from then on.

For about five weeks every year from July to August, we would open in a field situated in the centre of the holiday camps in Weymouth. In the August of that year ten years after his beloved wife had died, Richard Townsend, now frail at 94-year old, passed peacefully to rest. Because the family were not far away from the Chickerell yard, they laid Richard's body out in his wagon then towed it from the fairground to yard in Putton Lane, so that his funeral cortege could be started from the yard.

On hearing over the wireless of the death of Mr Richard Townsend, I went to Weymouth to express my sympathy and to see if I could be of any service to the family of this grand old gentleman.

Mr Townsend first became ill at Chard (Somerset) May fair. At 94, he must have been one of the oldest members of the Showmans' Guild, if not the oldest. I have had the privilege of knowing Mr Townsend and his family for 22 years; I have been particularly interested in how they quietly go about their business, and at no time seeking the limelight.

The last time I had the pleasure of talking to Mr Townsend was at Portland Fair in November 1959. When I must have spent an hour in his company talking about the old days. In my report at the time, I commented on the physical and mental fitness of this grand old showman.

A gentleman from Somerset had once written this tribute him:

Ah! Richard Townsend,
Will you go to Sutton Club
At the end of Whitsun week?
Will the kids all be riding on your Noah's Ark and
Will the lights be shining brightly long after dark,
When we have parted with our pennies,
You will pack up and then pull out
And take your swings and fairings.
To other scenes no doubt.
Till the golden tints of autumn
Give place to winter sere,
Then come again next summer
As you've done for many a year.

Death of 'The Guv'nor' at Weymouth

WELL-KNOWN throughout the West Country, Mr. Richard Townsend, whose death was announced in the "Echo" yesterday, remained up to his death at the age of 94, head of the firm of Richard Townsend and Sons, amusement caterers.

Mr. Townsend, who died ten days after the death of his 13-year-old granddaughter Joan, made his headquarters at Weymouth more than 60 years ago.

G.O.M. OF SHOWMEN'S GUILD

Believed to be the oldest active member of the Showmen's Guild of Great Britain and Ireland, he was known to everyone as "The Guv'nor." He was a beach tenant of Weymouth Corporation in the days of Queen Victoria, and the firm still has children's amusements on the beach.

Mr. Townsend was born in the business—it was founded by his father—and devoted his whole life to it. When he first came to Weymouth he operated a fairground on sites near where the Sidney Hall now stands. Later he ran a permanent fairground for many years in Commercial-road.

HIT BY WARS BUT SURVIVED

The firm was badly hit by the two world wars, but survived through these difficult times to get on its feet again in the post-war years.

Although in his nineties, Mr. Townsend travelled to fairgrounds in many parts of the West up to a short time before his death. And although he was taken ill at Chard Farm in May, he continued to travel to other fairs between then and the time he died. The headquarters at Weymouth is at The Depot, Putton-lane, Charlestown.

The funeral tomorrow will be at Weymouth-avenue Cemetery, Dorchester, where his wife, Mrs. Kate Townsend, was buried ten years ago.

Mr. Townsend is survived by four sons, two daughters and six grandchildren.

DEATH OF MR. RICHARD TOWNSEND

Believed to be one of the oldest active members of the Showmen's Guild, if not the oldest, Mr. Richard Townsend, head of the firm of Messrs. Richard Townsend and Sons, amusement caterers, died at Weymouth on Wednesday, August 10, at the age of 94.

He was known to fair-ground travellers and fans as "The Guv'nor."

TREASURED MEMORIES OF
JOAN
THE DEARLY BELOVED CHILD OF
ALBERT AND PHYLLIS
TOWNSEND
WHO FELL ASLEEP
28TH JULY 1965 AGED 14 YEARS

AN ANGEL IN THE BOOK OF LIFE
WROTE DOWN AN INFANT'S BIRTH
THEN CLOSED AND HE CLOSED
THE BOOK
TOO BEAUTIFUL FOR EARTH

GOODNIGHT
JOAN
LOVE.

At this time the family experienced two bereavements close together, sadly, we also lost Joan Townsend who was only thirteen years old at the time and was the fourth generation like my self

CHAPTER 16

1989; All Sold But We Still Have Our Memories

I have tried to draw a picture of a way of life that seems to fascinate many people. In years to come our future generations will start to wonder about their roots and it will all be here for them to read. So, how would I describe our way of life? Do not think for one minute it was a glamorous one. In the early years, in the beginning, William Townsend only got his little ride because he needed the money to survive after he lost his job on the Mail stagecoach. His son, Richard, due to a lack of education, continued in the business like his father, as it was only life he knew.

Then, as Richard and Kate's children (the third generation) were born, travelling around had become a way of life and Richard's children later had to work hard. Although it may sound romantic today, during my father's time steam travel on the road was slow and hard. They were not happy days, so much so that my dad, Joe, never wanted to talk much about his young days. We, the fourth generation, have continued to follow on in this life as, again, it was the only life we knew, or wanted to know for that matter. It has been our family's way of life for so long, that travelling is in our blood. From the very beginning, in William's day, there have been times of hardship in our business but still we carry on.

From an early age we all did something within the business. As soon as we could, we were taught how to serve and count the change and I would help bag up the money for the bank even before I could read. As for education, due to our father's occupation, we only went to school when we were able, which was from November to April. I can remember at school a careers teacher said to me in a polite manner "*Your life has already been mapped out for you*". How true that was! Over the years, Richard and Kate's children have gradually passed away and only their second born, Tom remained. He became the sole owner of Richard Townsend & Sons and the fourth generation took care to see that all carried on as usual.

In 1989, due to his age and health, a large amount of the business was sold to a dealer. Life moves on sometimes without you realising it. I wish I had recorded more stories of years ago, as when the older generation dies they take their memories and stories with them and they are lost forever.

However, with the help from two remaining elder members of my family who can remember, I have tried to ensure that, through this book, my family's memories will continue to live on. Now that all the rides and things we were brought up with have gone, I wish I had taken more notice of what we had, and savoured every moment of it. What I would not give to go back in time for just one day with all the family together again! My advice to any showmen now is, "Treasure every moment of today, as all could be gone tomorrow".

What I do know is that I have had the privilege to have lived such a life which I would not change for anything on this Earth. I was once told what we did yesterday makes us who we are tomorrow. That is so true when it comes to my family.

My Family

My daughters, Victoria (left) and Joe

Ancestors

If you could see your ancestors all standing in a row,
Would you be proud of them,
Or don't you really know?

Some strange discoveries are made when climbing family trees,
Some of them do not particularly please,
If you could see your ancestors all standing in a row,
There may be some you would not like to know.

But there is another question,
That requires another view,
If your ancestors were looking back,
Would they be proud of you?

(Author unknown)

100

I would like to thank my family and friends who have helped with the information and photographs in this book, including my cousin, Denny Cave and my husband, David Castlemain, for his patience throughout. Without their help, it would not have been possible.

Also, I would like to thank:

Douglas Dench, particularly for his research of the history and dates in Chapter 1

Stephen Smith and the Fairground Heritage Society for information and pictures in Chapters 1 & 2

Peter Legg, for engine details

Mr & Mrs Brian Burden, for their help in Chapter 5 (Steam and Our Queen)

Brian Andrews, for Chapter 12 (Dodgem's) and for the use of the pictures taken by the late Alan Imber
and Shane Seagrave, for his proof-reading of the manuscripts.

Every care has been taken to ensure that the material in this book does not infringe copyrights.

For further orders
kay58@fsmail.net
07784733398